Practice Makes Perfect

Practice Makes Perfect!

The Professional's Guide to Sales Success

by
Marvin E. Montgomery

(with George A. Becker)

Oakhill Press
Akron, Ohio & New York

Practice Makes Perfect

Library of Congress Cataloging-in-Publication Data

Montgomery, Marvin E., 1950-
    Practice Makes Perfect: The Professional's
    Guide to Sales Success / Marvin E. Montgomery with
George A. Becker. -- 1st ed.
    160 pp. X cm
    ISBN 1-886939-02-0
    1. Selling.
    I. Becker, George A., 1944-.   II. Title.
HF5438.25. M64   1995
658.85--dc20   95-24239
                          CIP

0 9 8 7 6 5 4 3 2 1

FIRST EDITION

First Printing, September 1995

Practice Makes Perfect

Contents

Acknowledgments

I got my "M.B.A.," I'm proud to say, from J.B. Robinson Jewelers.

So many committed individuals there left a mark on me personally as well as professionally. From company founder and chief executive officer Larry J.B. Robinson himself, to Larry Pollack, to Don Geller, Jim Mix, Sidney Greenberger, and Sandy Scott. Thank you.

They introduced me to the philosophy of preparing and practicing. From their experience, I saw how it became a culture, and that culture spawned a successful, dynamic company.

From their wisdom, I acquired the foundation to launch my own business, to have the opportunity to share such an enriching philosophy with others.

I would be remiss if I overlooked my friends Hal Becker, Adele Malley, and Carol Rivchun. They inspired me to write this book. I have taken their comments on earlier drafts to heart. And special thanks to Roger Herman for putting the pressure on me to finish it.

Nor could I have accomplished this project, ultimately, without the support and patience of my own family. It is to them I dedicate this book.

Chapter 1

INTRODUCTION

As a youngster, I marveled at my father's huge tool box. It always seemed larger than life. It was filled with every conceivable gadget--wrenches and hammers, screwdrivers and saws. Every time he opened that box, he always picked the right tool.

Successful selling is no different. Great sales professionals use the right "tools" to their advantage. Over the years, this strategy has allowed them to be successful.

This book will introduce the right set of sales tools for you, too.

They will aid you in every conceivable sale. They will help you, regardless of the product or service you sell, or the number of years you have been selling.

I write from experience.

I have observed and trained people in all aspects of sales at companies and organizations across the country for more than a quarter century. Few are aware of what sales tools to use and when to use them. If they are familiar with some, they seldom use them. Instead, most are foolish enough to <u>practice on their customers.</u>

They assume a huge risk. The time which prospective buyers have to make decisions has never been shorter, nor has their power of concentration been more distracted.

Customers no longer listen to what *you* want to tell them. Instead, *they* want to know if your product or service will fit their specific need. Not much more.

The point is, the unprepared salesperson never gets a second chance.

Believe me, the pressure to sell successfully will intensify. Surprised? Corporate "down-sizing" or "right-sizing" will continue. So will takeovers and mergers. The number of prospective customers will decline. In turn, your closing rate must increase.

You cannot take selling for granted. You cannot waste a sales opportunity. The stakes are rising. The field is shrinking. The competition is growing.

Customers have less loyalty to one particular company these days. Cynically, in today's business climate, customers listening to a sales pitch only want to know: "What's in it for me?"

So it becomes your responsibility to create a sense of loyalty among your customers.

Yet it baffles me that so many of us sell as if nothing has changed. Even though we make our living based on selling, we practice on our customers. We "run through" a presentation in front of them. We "rehearse" in their presence or over the telephone.

Can you imagine a doctor practicing during an operation? Or an attorney training before a jury and a judge? Or a firefighter putting out a blaze by trial and error? Yet salespersons practice on their customers all the time.

They are unprepared. They sustain an image that salespeople are fast-talking and aggressive, and that their main goal is to tell you what you want to buy and then talk you into it. Unfortunately, this stereotype affects all of us.

We don't have to cope with this image any longer.

This book will provide all the communication tools you will need to be a professional. With these tools, you will improve your sales presentation. You will confidently handle and overcome customer objections. You will increase your closure rate. You will expand your referral base.

You will, most of all, increase your profits. Whether you work in sales, customer service, or management, these tools will help you and your company or organization.

Remember, selling isn't a job.

It's a profession. The best salespeople understand this essential fact.

They are successful because they can create relationships with prospective or current customers. These relationships lead to business--and to repeat business.

You may already be aware of this reality. Only you may need encouragement to reach this goal.

This book will help you achieve that result. It will teach you how to practice effective, competitive selling skills every day. It will help you to sharpen those skills so you will use them all the time.

People always ask me how I recognize professionals. I always give the same answer. They ask and listen. They believe that selling is more than just a job. For them, it's a profession.

Professional salespeople always know the right sales tools to use during a presentation. They are totally familiar with them.

By the end of this book, you will understand them, too.

These 10 professional sales tools are:

1. A detailed knowledge of your company and its products or services.

2. An ability to greet customers and establish rapport.

3. An ability to ascertain the need for your products or services.

4. An ability to present your products' or services' features and benefits in an informative manner.

5. An ability to overcome objections and recognize genuine "buying signals."

6. An ability to close a sale.

7.   An ability to introduce "add-on" sales
         opportunities.

8.   An ability to reaffirm a sale, so your customers
         understand they have made the right buying
         decision.

9.   An ability to know when to turn over
customers   to a sales associate and

10.   An ability to handle difficult customers.

         The following chapters will cover each of these
tools. They feature examples so you will know when
to use them, *and* they have exercises so you can
practice applying them.

         When you begin to use them, you will
experience immediate and sustained improvement in
your ability to find out what a customer wants. Then
you will be able to provide it.

         Most important, you will never again practice
on your customers.

Chapter 2

The Value of Practice

Remember when you first learned to ride a bicycle? A parent or a loved one probably first told you how much fun you would have once you mastered your balance. Someone demonstrated the proper form and technique for riding a bicycle while their knees knocked against the bottom of the handlebars.

Now it was your turn. With their assistance, you climbed on. You pushed the pedals. There you were, moving. But you needed someone to walk beside you so you didn't fall. It had to be done in a controlled environment to minimize your injuring yourself.

Gradually, you began to steady yourself in spite of tipping. But someone was always at your side. The person helped you get back on. They encouraged you to continue until that wonderful moment when off you rode--alone.

But your progress was not left to chance. You were encouraged to practice. Someone made it a point to monitor your improvement. You were observed without your realizing it. You were watched as you walked your bike across a street. Someone wanted to make sure that when you did ride, you were doing it correctly.

When you handled yourself properly, you were praised. If not, you were called back in to practice again. No matter how long you had that bike, the reinforcement continued.

It's no different when you learn selling skills. Or when you want to improve skills you already have.

First, as a member of a company or an organization, top management must provide you with the proper training. Just like the person who taught you how to ride a bicycle.

Second, your trainer demonstrated how they would like you to perform the skill or technique.

Third, you were allowed to do it yourself--in a controlled environment. Your progress was monitored. You were given constructive feedback, including praise and reinforcement. Someone made sure to periodically follow up with you. You received continual training.

In the world of selling, this routine should be no different. Your managers must hold you and your associates accountable for improving your selling skills. They must allow you to regularly practice these skills until you have mastered them. Then the training becomes on-going.

1. Instruction

2. Demonstration

3. Practice in a controlled environment

4. Monitor

5. Follow-up

6. Re-enforcement training (on-going)

Preparation and practice are the keys to acquiring new selling tools.

As someone I once trained told me, in quoting his son's high school coach, "You practice during the week so you are able to compete at the meet!"

Yet it's easier to learn something new than it is to change a behavior. It's tough to begin to practice a simple, new communication in selling. Or in changing a selling technique, especially if we have been doing it for years.

For example, how many of us ask customers *before* they decide whether to buy?

"Would you like to..." or "Do you want to...?"

Your asking puts you at a selling disadvantage. It sets you up for a "no." It will lead to a loss of important business. But we do it in any event.

It starts with our need to ask permission, a disposition we acquired with age. As newborns, we never asked permission *about anything*. Our howling attracted the attention of grownups. They comforted and fed us.

But gradually as we got older, we learned behavior that was acceptable in the home, in the classroom, and on the playground. Or else, goodness knows, we would have turned into uncivilized misfits!

This behavior became deeply ingrained in us. So when our need to ask permission re-emerges, it will hinder the turning point in a sale.

I am not a psychologist. I am a professional sales trainer. I have several objectives in writing this book. I want to help you identify habits that limit your success in selling. I want to help you learn successful communication skills and selling techniques. And I want you to feel comfortable when you practice these skills and techniques.

Now let's reevaluate that turning point in a sale.

A much better response would be: "That sounds like a good decision."

This response assumes your customer has already decided to buy. But if the person is still undecided, it psychologically commits the individual to your viewpoint. You won't have to ask for the order. It will drop in your lap.

Another tactic is getting individuals to use their own name in a greeting.

I just wish one receptionist I've known for years could realize this truth. However, in spite of my efforts, she still throws up her hands and says:

"Oh, Marvin, why do we have to do it this way? What's wrong with the old way?"

Another example involves an experienced salesperson. No matter what I do to remind him, the individual will always ask a customer:

"Can I help you?"

He knows he should replace that phrase with "Good morning," or "Thank you for shopping here."

In spite of our best intention, wrong or obsolete habits will affect our productivity in sales.

Ample study supports this viewpoint.

Bruce R. Joyce and Beverly Showers, two prominent researchers, have analyzed the impact of training and practice on altering behavior. Their conclusions are that it requires practicing new information at least 13 times before someone can learn to communicate it competently. They also found that someone must practice a new behavior at least 113 times before changing it.

No wonder we resist change!

Yet we will have to change if we want to sell better. Our financial livelihood is at stake.

But before we can begin, we must learn the first principles of practice.

Saturday-morning staff meetings at Cleveland's J.B. Robinson Jewelers were devoted to more than checking inventory. Company managers used the opportunity to familiarize new employees with the retail jewelry business. They introduced new products. The highlight of the morning was when we assumed the role of either a store associate or a customer.

Chief executive officer Larry J.B. Robinson often practiced various roles, ranging from a "customer" to a salesperson in front of the group. This role was a challenge because of Larry's skill and ingenuity.

We would cover every imaginable realistic sales situation, utilizing the 10 sales tools I have just introduced. One time one of us would be an upset "customer." Another time someone would have trouble choosing a particular setting.

We reviewed our communicating. Throughout the morning, not without a hint of embarrassment, we would give constructive feedback on each individual's performance.

I learned a great deal from these sessions. They provided an enormous amount of practical, "hands-on" experience.

Later, I was promoted to director of training. I was in charge of developing the sales and customer-service expertise of more than 1,200 associates in 95 stores across several states. I took advantage of what

I had learned during those Saturday mornings. It helped me train our associates.

When I assumed that new position, I modified my sales-training philosophy. I no longer used the concept of role-playing. I began to use the word *practice*.

I gave emphasis to the benefits *of preparation and practice*.

Role-playing can turn off participants. Practice does not. Role-playing reminds me of what I did in elementary school. I stood in front of bored classmates. I tried to recite a poem without much success. It was an agonizing experience.

All of us had a similar experience. So when we played those roles on Saturday mornings with Larry, many of us had some momentary discomfort. When we stood in front of the group, it briefly reminded us of that experience in elementary school when we faced our classmates.

But each one of us recognized that practice was a simple concept to grasp. We knew that practicing would prove beneficial to our careers.

For example, most of us know that if we hope to get better at something, we need to practice, not play a role. This perspective applies to learning the game of golf or singing in a choir.

So in my training, I created the opportunity for us to practice. My associates told me they preferred this approach. The results proved this point. Individual sales increased steadily. The program was considered a success. Years later, when I meet some of my former Robinson associates, they still rave about the benefits of practice.

I encouraged everyone to practice individually and in groups. I made sure they practiced *properly*. I held them *accountable* for practicing. If I hadn't, many of them would have been tempted to give up. It's human nature.

For example, I work out regularly at a fitness club. Without fail, I see someone misuse exercise equipment. As a result, the person will not improve in spite of the exertion and expense. In time the individual probably will try another machine. Or quit working out entirely.

Fortunately, I had a personal trainer, Jeff Levine. For three weeks, Jeff supervised my workouts. He taught me to understand the function of each exercise machine. He explained the fundamentals. Later, he introduced advanced techniques.

Now I can set each machine for a particular exercise. I derive maximum benefit when I use the equipment. My stamina and conditioning have improved.

Jeff was my "drill sergeant." He held me accountable for exercising properly. He *"inspected"* my workouts and *"expected"* me to practice.

I call this approach "inspecting while expecting."

Jeff *expected* improvement. I didn't want to let him down. I didn't want to let myself down.

Selling is no different. Practice without accountability will impair selling just as much as no practice.

For example, I worked with a receptionist who had responsibility for answering the telephone. Supervisors frequently criticized her. They said she improperly handled calls.

I took a closer look at the company. I found that no one had taught her to answer the telephone properly. Unfortunately, she had received no guidance.

I met with her managers. I told them that until she was taught the company's telephone procedures, they had no business criticizing her.

"Why," I asked, "be upset with her, or anyone in your organization, if you haven't given her the proper tools?"

Once they recognized this oversight, they worked with her. They taught her proper procedures. They practiced them together. In no time, complaints about her work stopped.

When I begin working with a company, I gain management's endorsement of my training programs. This commitment provides accountability, the necessary first step for ultimate success. Associates know they will be held accountable if they fail to practice my sales techniques. Or if they practice them improperly.

They understand they must never quit. If they do, their managers will hold them accountable.

Remember: Practice is just a first step.

No one can become a complete golfer in one afternoon. The game is too complicated and frustrating. It requires regular and frequent practice.

In selling, you must practice regularly *before* you face your customers. Don't use the trial and error method on your customers. If you do, you will waste your time--and theirs.

The following guidelines will help you and an associate develop proper practice routines.

Review this list of the Benefits of Practice

1. Practice gives you an opportunity to identify strengths and weaknesses before you serve your customers.

2. Practice reinforces concepts of selling, enabling you to incorporate them into your daily activity.

3. Practice is a quick and excellent way to learn corporate culture or to benefit from an associate's experience.

4. One-on-one practice is challenging--no pain, no gain. Develop confidence as you sharpen your selling skills.

Remember: Feedback has to be in this order:

1. Self-evaluation by the salesperson.

2. Feedback by the observer.

- What you thought the salesperson did well.

- What you would have said or done differently, if you had been the salesperson.

3. Finally, ask the receiver how he felt as the "customer."

One-on-One Practice

Establish an objective (or the topic to be practiced.)

1. In advance, identify one specific part of the sale as your objective for the session. Select a realistic scenario.

2. Explain the objective to associates before beginning practice.

3. Explain the reasons for practice and its benefits.

4. Set a time frame, and show a high sense of urgency.

Establish roles and responsibilities.

1. Who will be the sender (of information)?

2. Who will be the receiver? This person must be challenging.

3. Make sure the customer knows what role they will play and how challenging they should be.

4. A third person, if present, can be the observer. (If you have only two people, the receiver is also the observer.)

Take notes.

1. Don't trust your memory.

2. Customer and observers should take notes.

3. Look for what went well.

4. Look for anything you would have done differently if you were the sender.

Practice.

1. Keep the receiver and sender in their roles. Don't talk about it--DO it!

2. Make the practice challenging and as realistic as possible.

3. Every practice scenario does not need to have a happy resolution. In other words, the customer does not always buy. This result will force the salesperson to be even more creative.

Stopping and restarting.

1. Correct a bad habit as soon as it's noted. Don't wait.

2. Show the sender how a change in statement will
   change results.

3. Then have the sender redo that section, time permitting.

Feedback.

1. As soon as the objective is achieved, stop the practice.

2. First, let the sender say what he or she would do differently (self-evaluation).

3. Next, the observer should give feedback on what went well and then on anything he or she would have said or done differently as sender.

4. Every observer should stress the positive. Avoid excessive criticism.

The Trainer must listen.

1. Teach people to improvise a behavior, not to role-play.

2. To keep the objective clear, concentrate on one or two key points; or at most three.

3. If appropriate, provide an example yourself.

Summarize.

1. Ask the observers what they have learned.

2. Give an assignment for the day on the aspect of sales.

3. Emphasize the importance of retaining what was learned and of translating it to the customer setting to close more sales.

Remember, daily practice will:

1. Increase productivity.

2. Increase add-ons.

3. Increase profits.

4. Raise employee morale and reduce employee turnover.

5. Improve customer relations and attract repeat business.

6. Create more confident sales people, more enthusiastic sales people, more highly motivated sales people.

7. Give you an opportunity to identify your strengths and weaknesses before you serve the customer. (Make mistakes in practice.)

8. Reinforce the selling concepts while improving your ability to execute selling techniques.

9. Enable you to learn from others while passing on the corporate culture; you will receive years of experience, otherwise gained through trial and error, in a shorter time.

10. Let you break old habits overlooked in your daily activities.

Example:

Work on the postponement objection. The purpose is to increase your closure rate and your commissions. This will also save you and your customer time, especially if you are able to close on the first call. (See Chapter 7 for more on handling objections)

One person should be the salesperson (the sender) and another associate will be the "customer" (the receiver.) Let's pick it up where the customer says:

Customer: "Your product sounds interesting. But I would like to think about it."

Salesperson: "What exactly is keeping you from making a decision today?"

Customer: "I have to involve Mr. Smith before a final decision is made."

Salesperson: "Once we get Mr. Smith's 'okay' is there any other reason why we shouldn't move forward with this contract?"

Customer: "No. As long as Mr. Smith signs off on it."

Salesperson: "Let's see if we can get Mr. Smith to okay this right now."

Customer: "Okay. I'll call his extension and see if he's available."

When an objection is overcome, stop practicing.

Practice Agreement

I _____ will review what I
learned with my manager and practice/implement the
following skills:

Skills to be Practiced	Practice Date	Coach	Start Date
_____	____	_____	____
_____	____	_____	____
_____	____	_____	____
_____	____	_____	____
_____	____	_____	____
_____	____	_____	____
_____	____	_____	____
_____	____	_____	____

Results:

I will share this practice agreement with my immediate supervisor.

Manager/Supervisor:

_____

Date Reviewed:

_____

Practice Log

NAME

DATE OF EMPLOYMENT

MANAGER

Topic	Date Read	Dates Practiced
Comments Trainers Completed Initial For Date Completion		With Trainer

Product Knowledge

Greet and Establish Rapport

Determining the Customer's Needs

Presenting Features and Benefits

Overcoming Objections

Closing the Sale

Add on Sales

Reaffirming the Sale

Turning Over

Handling Difficult Customers

Use this following worksheet for your practice sessions.

Sales Training
Observer Feedback
    Well
  Different

Chapter 3
Tool #1

Knowing Your Company and Its Products and Services

Every Saturday morning at J.B. Robinson Jewelers we covered another extremely important subject. We learned all we could about the company, its philosophy, its products, and its service.

We reviewed its policy about warranties and repair. We acquainted ourselves with new store locations. We went over job responsibilities. We got to know the history and philosophy of J. B. Robinson's.

We covered jewelry-related terminology. We tried to avoid technical jargon. We concentrated on making our answers intelligible.

Throughout the morning, we quizzed each other until we could easily recall this information. As we practiced, we became more motivated and enthusiastic.

The point was to prepare for any questions *before* our customers raised them.

Let's say you have just hired someone. Ask yourself what you would like that person to know and appreciate about your company and its products and services.

Or what you would say if your customer said:

"I have never heard of your company before." or "Please explain to me in more detail about your product or service."

Once you can complete this description, you will have mastered your first sales tool. Now you can communicate that information to your customers in a natural, professional manner.

You will be knowledgeable and professional.

Remember: Customers buy the *product* of your product or service. So the more you know about the company you represent, the greater the chance of sales success.

Practice Exercise:

I. Write down all the things that you feel a customer would want to know about your company.

Example:

1. Number of years in business.

2. Number of locations.

3. Form of ownership--family-controlled, for example.

4. Types of guarantees/warranties.

II. List the major products and services that you provide and develop a fact sheet on each one. Include features and benefits for each. (see Chapter 6 for more on this aspect)

III.Then practice communicating this information in a creative, conversational manner.

Practice Example

Customer:
"I've never heard of your company before."

Salesperson:
Give response
(Don't forget to start off with a question. So when you give your response, make sure it addresses your customer's concern.)

Customer:
"Tell me more about your product or service."

Salesperson:
Give response
(again, start with a question.)

Chapter 4
Tool #2

Greeting Customers and Establishing Rapport

On a daily basis, everyone in business scrambles for profits. Being unprepared in this costly endeavor jeopardizes one's financial survival.

Yet most of us practice on our customers, in spite of a shrinking base.

We fail to realize the impact of this "fly-by-the-seat-of-our-pants" habit of mind on our customers.

It makes those of us in sales appear unprofessional. It differentiates us from physicians, attorneys, teachers and firefighters. They practice.

They prepare. They train before they get a license to engage in their professions.

Yet sales is a profession where the necessity to practice is almost never required.

This lack of preparation shows. A simple greeting used during a sales call often will reveal how well prepared--how professional--we actually are.

Why do so few of us realize this essential detail?

For example, consider *how* you tell someone "Good Morning!" If it sounds stagnant, stale, or unenthusiastic, it will have an affect on your customer. If it lacks sincerity, it will reduce your time to sell.

But haven't we used this greeting thousands of times? For this reason, my advice is to shed greetings that *we* are comfortable in using. Instead, make it a point to fit your greeting to each customer.

Otherwise, your first impression will fall flat.

A greeting that is genuine, enthusiastic, creative and conversational will establish a sense of rapport with your customers. Genuine naturalness will make them feel at ease.

Remember! This is the foundation of your sale.

It will shorten a psychological "distance" between your customers and yourself. It will soften their fear that they are about to hear a high-pressured sales pitch. It will ease their worry. It will provide reassurance. It will make them comfortable with you and with what you have to sell.

It will build a lasting relationship.

Yet it amazes me that so many salespersons overlook the importance of their greeting. They seem to treat their customers as nothing more than "factors" in their next commission. They regard them as potential "dollar signs." They have that kind of attitude in spite of the enormous cost to market their products and services.

Next time you meet your customers, establish rapport.

When you walk into an office the first time, look around. If there is a golf club in the corner, ask about the person's handicap. If you spot a family picture on a credenza, use that object as an opener. If you pass construction in a hallway, or notice art on a wall, use the opportunity to "break the ice."

Find common ground--a mutual interest in sports, or in family pursuits, or in the weather.

Pay attention to every gesture. Become knowledgeable about reading the "language" of these gestures. Recognize responses from your customers-- their body signals--so you can adjust your comments, if necessary.

Someone's head tilted forward or sideways indicates receptivity. A face turned away, even slightly, is a "distancing." If a person's head is tilted back so his nose is looking down at you, well, I'm sorry to say, it's as negative as it sounds.

Rapid blinking or constriction of the pupils signals distress or disagreement. A stare may be a challenge. Biting, or licking, lips shows discomfort.

Thinning of the lips is almost always a sign of a negative response, even if combined with a smile. A small or social yawn often does not signify boredom. But it usually indicates some level of discomfort.

A shrug, or roll of the shoulders, is a strong sign of receptivity or submission. Squaring them indicates a rigid, authoritarian attitude that could be mean difficulty if directed toward you.

Open palms are a universal sign of good will and receptivity. Clasping, or holding a finger, hand, arm or elbow in the other hand could imply the

person is thinking seriously about what you've said--
a positive sign.

A hand placed behind the head at the back of
the neck indicates squirming. Perhaps you are
making the person uncomfortable.

If someone leans toward you, that means a sign
of attention. But leaning back or angling the body
away is a cut-off. Drawing in the shoulders is a sign
of insecurity. So is folding--drawing the arms and
legs in toward the body.

Again, these are clues. As you recognize them,
you will be able to fit what you tell your customers.

But that ability is just one sales communication
tool.

Learning to paraphrase is another proven sales
technique. It is summarizing what a customer has
said.

It can be simple phrases such as: "What you
are saying to me is..." or, "If I understand you
correctly..."

Paraphrasing will improve your active
listening. Your customers will give you more
information that you can use later to your advantage.

Notice how often I use the word *you* in a conversation. Using "you" when you greet your customers indicates sincerity, a key element in building trust.

So will your making sure you do not rush to your presentation. The greeting and rapport that you will establish should be no different from what you would do if someone was visiting your home for the first time.

Welcome your customers. Make them feel at ease in your presence. Remember, establishing good relationships early on will establish your business.

These are the key ingredients in greeting customers and establishing rapport:

Greeting:
  Use your customer's name
  Shake their hand
  Convey a professional image
  Modulate the tone of your voice
  Maintain eye contact
  Show a genuine interest
  Put your customers at ease
  Paraphrase their comments or questions

Establishing rapport:

Convey positive body language
Learn to read language of gestures
Take notes

Practice Exercise:

Drills:30-second   60-second   90-second

A sender (salesperson) approaches a receiver (customer) using techniques described in this chapter. At first, take 30 seconds or less in practicing your greeting and establishing rapport.

When you have mastered a 30-second routine, move to 60 seconds and then 90 seconds. This practice will improve your ability to relax, it will put your customer at ease and, most important, it will allow a relationship to develop.

Note: Keep in mind that there is no time limit on your greeting & rapport. This is for practice only.

Chapter 5

Tool # 3

Determining the Need for Your Product or Service

Let's face it! Your ability to greet a customer and then establish rapport is crucial. But you must quickly accomplish something else. You must determine if there is a genuine need for the product or service you provide.

Making this transition requires a real sense of timing on your part. If you move too fast, you may appear insincere. However, if you move too slowly, you may run short of time.

So pace yourself as you begin to determine if there is indeed a need for your product or service.

If only the caller from a local chimney-sweeping company had that aim in mind. After spending several minutes with me over the telephone reading from a scripted list of questions, she then led up to the close:

"Since we'll be in your neighborhood next week, can we send someone by to check out your chimney?"

"Sorry to say that won't be possible," I said.

"Why's that," she asked.

"Because my home doesn't *have* a fireplace!"

"Oh, you don't? Oh, okay. Thanks. Bye."

If only her company had done its homework. It never would have called me in the first place. Its research already would have eliminated owners of homes without fireplaces. But even if it did have a telemarketer make a call, that person should first have been instructed to ask about my home's features.

It was the second time in two years I had heard from this particular company! Talk about wasted effort.

For this reason, I always like to find out from my customers if my services will match their needs. It saves me time. It saves my customers time.

If I had been representing the chimney-sweeper, I would have asked this question:

"Hi, I'm Marvin Montgomery. I'm calling from the Dust-In-My-Hair Chimney Sweep Company. Does your house have a fireplace?"

"No."

End of conversation.

I'm just like a physician. I must evaluate a patient's condition before I can make a diagnosis. Then I can prescribe the correct medicine.

You should do the same thing.

Before you can offer customers your particular product or service, you must determine their needs. You must understand their expectations. If possible, you must even get them to discuss their budget.

How do you begin?

By asking questions and by listening to your customers' answers. This approach will set you apart from your competition.

Or else, if you just talk about yourself and then tell about your company's products or services, it will be impossible to discover what your customers *really* need.

No matter how much you know about your product or how much experience you have, you will get off on the wrong sales footing. You will not be creative and conversational. Worst of all, you will sound robotic.

And your customers?

They will not respond. They will react-- negatively. You literally will have talked yourself out of a sale.

In order to avoid this, you must recognize that successful salesmanship starts with active listening.

It's a skill that requires constant practice. But as you practice, you will improve your capacity to concentrate.

It's not that we don't hear what our customers are telling us. But they rarely clarify their needs immediately. It takes time and effort to establish a rapport with your prospective customer.

Learn to sort your customer's comments. Mentally summarize them. Use them to anticipate the likely conclusion the person will draw. Don't forget to "read between the lines" for any nonverbal clues.

It is crucial that you listen actively. So is your body language. Take notes. Ask questions. If necessary, paraphrase. I like to jot down an occasional note. I never interrupt even during a pause. But I don't let things pass that I fail to grasp or understand. Take advantage of this interval between thinking and responding.

Occasionally, I nod or say, "Yes, I see." It conveys interest. I rephrase comments in the speaker's own terms. By doing so, I can think about a correct response. It shows the speaker I am following the conversation.

Developing a line of questioning is another invaluable tool.

It will improve your listening skills. It will help you gain and retain the initiative. You will control your conversation. In your questioning, you can reaffirm the rapport your greeting has already established. You can learn more about your customer's likes and dislikes. You will show you care without being pushy.

News reporters prefer to ask open-ended questions. They hope their interviewee will answer as expansively as possible.

Few customers can really articulate what they need in the first few minutes with a salesperson. In contrast, questions that elicit short answers may stifle a sales call.

Now it is time for you to practice how to determine your customer's needs, using effective listening and questioning techniques. First, make a list of questions that you should be asking during the assessment. Then practice them!

Remember:

Ask questions to gain and retain the initiative.

Ask questions to control the conversation.

Ask questions to appear pleasant and interesting.

Ask questions to adapt to the customer's individual traits.

Ask questions to clarify and elucidate, and

Ask questions to establish commitment.

These are open-ended questions, designed to have your customer provide expansive answers:

What..?

How...?

Who..?

Where..?

When..?

Why..?

These are direct questions, designed to elicit specific or precise answers:

Do you......................................?

Will you.....................................?

Have you...................................?

Most of all, do not sound robotic in your questioning and be extremely organized. Remember that your customers have limited time. So you must quickly focus on determining their needs.

Practice Exercise:

Start at the point during the sale when its time to find out what your customer wants done.

Salesperson: Using the questions you have developed, begin assessing you customer's needs. Be careful not to sound robotic or scripted.

Remember: You goal is to find out if there is a need for the products and services that you provide.

Chapter 6

Tool #4

Presenting the Features and Benefits of Your Product or Service

Sooner or later, *the* critical moment will arrive. Your customers will ask: "If you can't tell me what's in it for me, then why should I buy from you?"

Your answer must demonstrate exactly how your product or service will fit their needs.

First, can you describe the virtues of your company in 25 different ways? Or list 25 different features and benefits of your particular product or service? Or 20? Or 10? How about five?

It's not so easy, is it?

Many of us in sales know so little about what we sell. We aren't well-versed in our product knowledge. This ignorance makes it tough to handle customers' objections or questions, especially when our competition can.

Or we memorize that knowledge. Or we present that information as if we were reciting a "laundry list" of reasons to do business.

There is a difference between knowing something and memorizing something. I compare it to hearing a song for the first time. Once you know that song, then it becomes your song. You can sing it any way you want.

So don't memorize your presentation.

Instead, focus on only those features and benefits that your customers will be concerned about. Your learning the difference between memorizing details and knowing which details to mention will help you.

For example, your company may be 80 years old. That's an impressive feature. It suggests "staying power." If your customers care about staying power, your citing this fact will make an impact on your customers. It will establish your credibility.

Your product may have an exceptional warranty policy that surpasses what the competition offers. Don't forget to mention that policy, if you have determined that warranties are a priority with your customers.

The point of this particular action is to directly link the most appropriate features of your products and services to your customer's needs. And the only way to achieve this is by finding out what your customer wants done.

Surprised?

It's simple. If you choose your questions carefully, your customers' answers will guide you. If they are interested in quality, you can cite the appropriate features and benefits.

If turn-around time is important to them, then you can mention the speed and efficiency of your company in handling orders. If a guarantee policy or a comprehensive service agreement is a priority, you can address this issue.

One customer will value something about your product or service that another will not. No problem. Since you are familiar with every aspect of your line of work, your responses will always meet each customer's specific, immediate needs.

When you do, you will create lasting customer satisfaction.

An ideal way to focus on the features and benefits of your respective product or service is to list them. Then you must practice them so you know them.

First, write down the features and benefits of your company.

By matching a feature and a benefit to your customers' needs, you will save their time--and yours. You will be a professional.

Don't forget: Determining needs + presenting benefits = need satisfaction.

Practice testing yourself daily until you know every feature and every benefit.

Practice Exercise:

Test yourself by listing the features and benefits of your company--and then of your products and services.

Remember: You won't have mastered them until you can list them without hesitation. Set a time to do so. Then list them on a sheet of paper.

Features   **Benefits**

Then do it for your product or service.

Features   **Benefits**

Chapter 7

Tool #5

Overcoming Objections

"Your price is too high."

Who hasn't heard that response? How about this one?

"I need some time to think on it."

Such objections are part of every-day selling.

Welcome them; they are opportunities to meet the needs of your customers. Beads of sweat shouldn't appear on your brow or your palms.

Don't avoid eye contact. Don't drop your voice.

Be happy that objections surface. They present you with an opportunity to bring closure to a sale.

But, first, you must overcome these concerns immediately. If not, all your planning and preparation--and actual selling--will falter on the brink of potential success.

Sadly, statistics that track national trends reveal, it's a moment when ill-trained or unprepared salespeople stumble.

Some 75 percent of all those in sales fail to pursue a prospect after the first objection, an incredible misuse of their organization's or company's money and effort. Let's look at the price objection. Some sales people aggravate the situation by fishing for an answer. They will immediately assume that price is an objection. Completely unprepared to respond, they will even adjust the price.

Worst of all, they will lower it.

They will answer an objection in such a way that they will literally talk themselves out of a sale.

In contrast, why do the other 25 percent consistently produce nearly 95 percent of all sales?

It is because, these same statistics show, approximately 63 percent of all sales do not take place until the salesperson has overcome the buyer's *fifth* objection!

What perseverance!

Why is only one salesperson in four deemed successful?

It is because these motivated individuals have learned to recognize that objections are really excuses, or momentary detours, on the path to an ultimate sale.

They refuse to accept the notion that they may have encountered a sale's dead end.

From experience, they realize that a prospect is, in fact, emitting a crucial "buying signal."

Customers raise specific objections for all kinds of reasons even if they liked your presentation. Legitimately, they will tell you, they just aren't interested. Or it could be they feel uncomfortable in citing the real reason. They can't afford the price. Or someone else has the authority to buy.

Perhaps they need to feel reassured they are making the right choice. Or they don't fully understand the benefits of your product or service. Or they are asking for more information.

When they object, they are offering you another opportunity to showcase your product or service.

Your learning to deal with this inclination will enable you to take your selling skills to a higher, more productive level. It will bring results at a crucial moment. Otherwise, the sales opportunity will fail.

Regardless of the reason, your customer's objections offer important clues.

Once you have trained yourself to analyze them, you will be able to seize, or regain, the initiative at a crucial moment. Your responses will be authoritative and they will not be defensive-sounding. You will be perceived as sincere and in control.

You will come across as a professional. You can achieve this result because you have prepared and practiced a series of responses for objections you fully expect.

First, learn to differentiate the five categories of objections. Usually, in one form or another, they relate to price. Others reflect a subtle, personal reason that someone is uncomfortable in divulging. It could be that a particular feature of your product or service falls short of the competition's. It could be the competition that you're up against, or your customer may be postponing their decision. Look for objections which fall primarily into one of the following categories.

1. Price

2. Product/Service

3. Postponement

4. Personal

5. Competition

Next, never react. Instead focus your energy on getting the customer to respond, to clarify. The only way to do this effectively is by posing a question or paraphrasing the response.

For example, one approach is to ask:

"What makes you feel my price is too high?"

Another approach is: *"If I understand you correctly, Ms. Johnson, you're concerned you're not getting the best value for your money."*

Either approach will enhance your ability to determine the *real* reason for an objection. In fact, as you listen to the answer, it could be a multitude of reasons. Price. The fact that the buyer has a lower bid from another supplier.

The customer is testing the firmness of your price. The customer does not fully understand the product's benefits. The customer is experiencing "sticker shock" because it's been years since she last bought such a product.

So don't respond until you peel away the "surface" of an objection to uncover its core.

Proper practice and preparation will help. Have an answer for every conceivable objection--for price, speed of delivery, etc.

First, write down a series of anticipated objections. Then directly next to them, list your anticipated responses. Your practicing this exercise will enable you to know exactly what to say in any situation. It will eliminate surprise completely. It will lead to your asking for acceptance of the answer you have given.

In effect, you are attempting to make the person feel comfortable with your response.

If your customer says, *"Yes, I accept your answer,"* or *"Now I understand what you are talking about,"* then you can move to a trial close such as

"Fine, let's go forward," or *"Fine, I'll need your okay."*

But if the person rejects trial closes such as these, saying, *"Let me think it over,"* then repeat the process by stating:

"What exactly is keeping you from making a decision?"

Or if the person says, *"There's no money in the budget,"* paraphrase your response this way:

"Then this would be a perfect time to discuss it. I want to show you where right now you might be spending more than you need to and be getting lower quality results. Since your phone calls are based on gaining new customers, I'd like to show you how you can do this while increasing your productivity. Would Tuesday..."

Practice this process. You will handle objections better. You will recognize legitimate buying signals. You will satisfy your customer. You will, I predict, be able to close sales sooner.

Remember: An objection is an opportunity to bring closure to the sale. Customer are telling you their needs and concerns. They are asking questions to get answers.

So welcome them!

Remember: Objections usually fall into these five categories:

> Price.
> Product.
> Postponement.
> A Personal Reason.
> Competition.

In gathering your response, do the following:

1.   Ask a question or paraphrase.

2.   Answer.

3.   Ask for acceptance of the answer.

4.   Make a trial close.

Practice Exercise:

Start by making a list of the questions and objections that your customers ask during the sale and then brainstorm possible answers.

Practice these objections until you feel comfortable with your responses. Again, having one person taking the role of customer and another the salesperson, pick up the sale exactly where the objections occur and practice your responses. Use the four step process mentioned to uncover the real reason and trial closes.

OBJECTION

PRICE

PRODUCT

PERSONAL

POSTPONEMENT

COMPETITION

Chapter 8

Tool #6

CLOSING

At last, you're about to ask for the order. It's the culmination of a process that began with an inquiry or a lead. Then it was qualified. Then it was fully developed during a presentation of the product's or service's features and benefits.

But if we literally ask for a sale, we will make a mistake. Haven't we said we have to unlearn this acquired need of ours to ask permission?

Yet why do so many of us expend so much effort and expense and stumble at such a critical moment? It's as if we are waiting--naively---for a customer to say:

"I'll take it."

My experience in counseling companies across America confirms this phenomenon. Frequently I am asked to "shop" the competition. I call on scores of businesses that range from those engaged in manufacturing to others that dispense services.

Almost without exception, I encounter salespersons who make no effort to challenge me after I tell them: "Hmmm...let me think about it."

"Oh, okay," they respond. "I'll call you in a week or two."

Few ever say, "Excuse me, Mr. Montgomery, may I ask: 'What did you want to think about? Or what's keeping you from moving forward?'"

To my frustration, they hand me their business card. They ask *me* to call *them* if and when I am ready to buy.

Of course, they sincerely want my business. But they have the wrong priorities. Selling is their responsibility, not mine!

Their reluctance to challenge customers stems from a fear of rejection.

Which fear do you have? Will you feel guilty if you fail? Can't you handle rejection? Or if a customer turns you down, are you worried what you will have to tell your boss?

Do you want your customer to offer to buy? Do you feel awkward with only a few standard closes?

Well, what if you omitted a significant feature about your product or service? Is it too late to bring that up? Or could your price be too high?

All things considered, perhaps you should skip the close and make a graceful exit? Nonsense.

No salesperson I know has ever been killed by the word, "No!"

Each one of us should *want* to ask for the order, even if our customers put us off. For one thing, believe it or not, our customers expect us to do so. Our closing should follow what we have accomplished.

We have greeted our customers and have established a rapport with them.

We have determined, by asking questions and then listening, their true needs.

We have presented the appropriate features and benefits of our product or service.

We have answered their questions or objections.

We should want to know the reasons they choose not to buy from us. Once we do know these reasons, we can address them with the proper response. Furthermore, it will provide crucial guidance for every other sale.

It should be natural, then, for us to want to close. Without question, that is our mission. How else will we *ever* determine what the real resistance is? After all, in making a sale, don't we set out to eliminate barriers between our customers and ourselves? Until one hears these reasons, our selling will remain incomplete.

No honest, open communication can begin until we discover what's really frustrating our customers.

Unfortunately, so few of us understand this truth. We don't challenge our customers. We accept whatever they tell us. Not just in a sales call. It's a tendency that damages closure in even the simplest forms of communication.

Compare these responses to a customer's telephone inquiry:
"May I help you?"

"Yes, how much is an eye examination?"

"The exam is $19," the person is told.

"Thank you very much."

This example highlights selling by someone I call an *"Order Taker."* That person accepts--at face value--whatever customers tell them. Nothing else.

Compare that attitude with one displayed by what I call an *"Order Maker."* This salesperson sees opportunity in every customer contact.

"How much is an eye exam?"

"Will this be for glasses or contacts?"

"For contacts."

"Oh, congratulations! Is this your first pair?"

"Yes, it sure is. And, to tell you the truth, I'm kind of nervous about it."

"Oh, don't worry about it. Let me ask you something: I'm looking at my appointment book here; when's a good time for you to come in?"

"I can get in Tuesday morning."

"Great. We have you scheduled for Tuesday at 9 a.m. The eye exam will be $19, and we'll see you then."

With almost the same amount of energy, notice the difference. By asking and listening, the "Order

Maker" sets the stage for a sale. Nothing, I argue, will do more to improve your selling skills than your becoming aware of these dynamics.

Practice them until you use them naturally.

Everyone in your company or organization, regardless of their job description, will benefit. One client told me the successful closing rate of one of his company's technicians rose 10 percent, to nearly 80 percent. This person, when given the opportunity, no longer was afraid to ask for the order. The individual had practiced techniques to respond properly to customers' concerns.

I like to challenge my clients.

I want them to imagine what would happen to their companies if each of their sales people would close just one more sale in a day or in a week.

The rewards would be enormous.

When I appear before their sales organization, one of the first things I do is ask the attendees about their last sales experience. I want them to tell me if they know who was responsible for closing. I ask them when, in that communication, the first attempt was made to make that all-important closure.

I wish I had an over-abundance of success stories to convey. Few, if anyone, in the audience can recall how they closed.

Talk about lack of preparedness. How would we like it if our surgeon told us, in response to a question, "Hey doc, how did you operate on me?" "I don't know. I guess I was lucky."

But the fact is that surgeon was trained to know exactly what he was going to do in every step of that procedure. He left nothing to chance.

The same discipline should apply to everyone in sales. Never should you have to ask yourself: "What do I do now?"

Just like that surgeon, salespeople should know what to do in each step of selling--from establishing rapport to achieving closure.

All of us should want to make the close. Deep down, as professionals, we really do care about our customers. That sentiment was one of the reasons for our calling on them. We sincerely want them to benefit from our product or service.

Even if that sale should ultimately elude us, we can still use closure to our advantage. Empathetic prospects will respect us for asking for the order. They will become a referral source.

Let's face it: There are no half-closes. Either you close a sale or you don't.

Here are 12 recommended closes. They are adapted from the thinking of J. Douglas Edwards, a nationally respected authority on selling.

Practice them so you can easily fit one to any sales situation.

Close #1: The Order Blank

Question each of your customers. Every professional salesperson uses this approach. It creates an opportunity to complete order blanks, contracts, agreements--various closing forms. Professional salespersons feel that as long as their customers continue to answer each question, they will eventually buy.

At that moment *don't* say: "Now sign this!"

Instead, use: "Would you okay this for me, please?"

Close #2: The Alternative Choice

Provide several alternatives -- "deluxe or standard;" "white or gray;" "cash or credit." But start each phrase this way: "Which would you prefer?"

Close #3: The Free Trial

Want to sell a puppy? Let the customer take one home overnight. This close is effective, especially with children or neighbors. They can become so enthralled they will make it impossible for the prospect to bring the puppy back.

Close #4: The Ben Franklin Balance Sheet

The perfect close for an indecisive buyer. Draw a line down the middle of a piece of paper. On one side list the reasons favoring the purchase. List those that could block it on the other.

Benjamin Franklin, so the story goes, did this with great success. So do many sales people. Since they know their product and service, their *yes* column always has more points beneath it than the negatives under the *no* side. By showing this sheet to their customers, salespersons will have something substantial to support their close.

Close #5: The Call Back

Sometimes getting closure at the first meeting is impossible. So make it your business to close an appointment or to call back within a few days, a potentially risky move. Often, in this instance, customers are still unwilling to commit. So, as a way to improve your chances, when you do speak, try to introduce an idea that stimulates interest. It could be something relevant but new.

Then say: "As you remember, we agreed that..." That response will enable you to move straight into your closing sequence, making it unnecessary to ask if your customers have had a chance to think it over.

Close #6: The New "Lost" Sale

Deploy this close when everything you have tried so far has failed. As you depart, stop, turn around and, borrowing from a classic sales line, tell your customers:

"Pardon me, sir. I wonder if you would help me for a moment." Then, as sincerely as possible, offer an apology--for not making the sale.

"Since I make my living in sales, would you mind telling me what I did that was wrong so that I don't make the same mistake again?"

Surprisingly, if you establish credibility with this close, you will get your sale.

Close #7: The Secondary Question

Let's say you're selling an intangible business service.

First ask: "As I see it, sir, the only decision you have to make today is this: Do you want this for the two-year or the three-year term?" Immediately continue: "And, by the way, do you want to use your pen or mine?"

Once your customers makes this minor decision (the pen), they automatically will decide the major one.

Close #8: The Sharp Angles

When customers have specific questions about your product, respond by asking: "Do you want it if it does?"

When customers answer *yes*, you will have made your sale based on proof. This close is known as "sharp angling." If you don't do it, you will not get confirmation or the sale.

Close #9: The Final Objection

What if customers answer your close with an objection and then another? Don't panic. Listen. Expand upon it. Confirm the objection. Question it. Answer it. Then confirm the answer and close it by saying, "Now that completely settles it, doesn't it?"

Close #10: The "I'll-Think-It-Over"

"Let me think it over." Instead of letting that thought go unanswered, turn it into a specific objection which you can handle.

Respond this way: "That's fine. Obviously you wouldn't take your time thinking it over unless you were really interested, would you? I'm sure you're not telling me this just to get rid of me, so may I assume you will give it careful consideration?"

Customers, thinking you're going to let them go, agree. Now you can say: "Just to clarify my thinking, what phase of this program is it that you want to think over? Is it this aspect...or is it that aspect...?" By doing this without pausing you will clear away any final objection and land the sale.

Close #11: The Question

Suppose customers ask: "Will I get 30-day delivery?" Instead of saying *yes*, create a closing by asking, "Do you want it in 30 days?" When customers say *yes*, they have made a purchase. This simple close has countless applications and is too effective to ignore.

Close #12: The Similar Situation

Refer to third parties--customers who did--or did not--use your product or service. This close will allow your prospect to identify with success, especially if the customer is in a similar business or industry. Use this third-party reference just before you summarize benefits. This approach allows you to expand each one of them. It allows your customers to identify with them, too.

Familiarizing yourself with each of these suggested closes will assist you in selling. Practicing them will improve your rate of success.

Most of all, remember that every sale, either through verbal or written commitment, must be closed!

Let's review.

A Direct Close: How did you want to handle the balance?

An Either/Or Close: Did you want two cases or three?

An Assumptive Close: It sounds like you have made a decision. Let's go over to the counter and write up the contract.

List additional closes that are appropriate for your industry.

Practice Exercise:

Using objections as the scenario, practice some of the closing phrases you have listed.

The customer should say no several times, so the salesperson will be challenged to use several different closes.

Chapter 9

Tool #7

Introducing "Add-On" Opportunities

I'll be blunt. "Add-on" sales will increase your business by as much as 20 percent.

In fact, I guarantee it. "Add-on" sales from the products or services you offer will maximize your bottom line. Most of all, these additional sales will deepen customer allegiance. They will create repeat business and referrals.

Unfortunately, most salespeople overlook this potential source of business. They just don't pursue it. Some only occasionally solicit added sales. Others, I discover, even let their *customers* ask about different products or services.

This approach is foolish. It is unprofessional.

Always seek additional sales opportunities. If not, your customers will direct their business to someone else. Instead of your building sales, you will jeopardize them.

Introducing "add-on" sales should follow from what we have already covered. For example, you can offer your customers additional products or services because you have asked and listened. You have assessed their needs. Now you will know what "add-ons" they will require, which "add-on" services or products will best meet their needs.

Just as important, you will come across as a professional. Your customers will listen to your recommendations. In your customers' eyes, you will be seen as an "order maker," not an "order taker."

Need motivation?

During your annual physical examination, your physician reads an X-ray. He notices a spot on your lung. But he decides to withhold this information. He fears that if he divulges this dramatic news, you will think he wants to increase his fee.

Nonsense!

You *expect* him to divulge this information. He is morally and professionally obligated to do so.

You buy several gallons of paint at a hardware store. But a salesperson fails to ask if you need anything else. Once you return home, you realize you should have purchased several additional items. These are rollers, thinner, drop cloths and a step ladder. Without them, you cannot finish the project.

But you don't return to the hardware store where you purchased the paint. Instead, you choose to buy these additional products from another retailer closer to home. It will save time.

The salesperson at the first store was just an "order taker." He was content to sell paint and nothing else. So, for these accessories, you took your business elsewhere.

Regard every customer as a source of additional business. Ask for this additional business. Ask for referrals who might have similar needs. Don't worry what impact "add-on" opportunities will have on your original sale.

It's your responsibility to inform your customers about any additional products and services you provide.

You're a sales professional.

You are obligated to take this approach. You will not be perceived as overbearing. Nor will you appear as though you are trying to trick or manipulate your customers into making an unnecessary purchase.

Remember, customers will buy to satisfy a need. They also will buy to satisfy a want. So don't narrow your selling unnecessarily.

What you really will be doing is satisfying *all* of your customers' needs. You will overlook no sales opportunity. Your customers will value your professionalism.

"Didn't you say, sir, you are about to paint a bedroom?"

"Well, yes I am," the customer will reply.

"Well, then, may I suggest that you look at our accessories, so you can pick up what you need while you are here in our store? Brushes? Thinner? Cloths? A ladder? We have what you need. I'd be happy to show them to you right now."

You are assisting your customers in making good, sound buying decisions. You are making certain that no sales opportunities slip by. You are preventing someone else from coming in and selling a competitive product or service, to your ultimate disadvantage.

The more selling you do, the less fall-off in business will you experience. You will build long-term business relationships. You will have new opportunities to provide a total package of your products or services.

One way to start is by completing the following exercise:

List Your Major Companion Products or Services	List Your Products or Services

Total $_____

Now compare this dollar amount with your actual sales. What is the potential for improving your average sale? When you can determine this amount, you will be able to increase your new sales potential.

Practice Exercise:

As a salesperson, make an assessment of each potential sale. Then suggest any additional products or services that are needed--or wanted--by a customer.   Make successful selling a part of all practice sessions so that it becomes a habit.

Chapter 10

Tool #8

Reaffirming the Sale

Customers almost always have second thoughts once they've purchased a product or service. The longer they have to wait for a particular purchase to arrive, for example, the more likely they will be to cancel the original order.

Or they will stop payment on a check.

Everyone is susceptible to "buyer's remorse."

We're prone to talking ourselves out of a purchase moments after we've made one.

"Maybe I should have first checked with my wife?"

"Did I spend too much?"

"Am I getting ripped off?"

If a customer's own remorse doesn't doom a sale, neighbors and business associates can complicate the situation. Often, these parties are well-known for their unsolicited second-guessing.

"What possessed you to buy that in the first place?" they will ask.

Fortunately, as sales professionals, you now can deploy several useful tools to reassure your customers that their purchasing decision was indeed a wise one. Each one will remove the slightest doubt in their mind. It will reaffirm their purchase in a forceful, positive way.

Even before customers leave your presence, or hang up the telephone, it is imperative for you to make sure you support their purchase unequivocally. Avoid the trap of inadvertently planting a kernel of doubt that, over time, can fester.

"By the way, if you ever have any problems, give me a call."

Will that build trust and confidence? Hardly. Instead, you should say:

"I'm here; you have made the right choice. You will be very pleased with you decision. I look forward to seeing you again."

Next, make it your business to review the features and benefits of the product or service that was purchased. Cite warranties and other guarantees. Let customers know you will be available--*all the time*--should they need to contact you about anything.

Another crucial tool is deploying what I term the "anticipatory set."

Tell customers that you will be calling them at a specific date. This approach will serve them well if they hear negative comments, or if they have to wait a substantial amount of time between date of purchase and actual delivery.

After the sale, actively maintain your customer-salesperson relationship. Don't let customers feel they will never hear from you again. Call them. Find opportunities to see them.

Make them think about your product or service. If not, they will forget about you. Then, when they need to purchase something, they will turn to the person they perceive to be there--your competitor, not yourself.

I fondly recall the surgeon who operated on my foot more than 15 years ago. Not content to let his office staff call me the morning after my surgery, he surprised me. He stopped by my house to chat. It only took a few minutes.

But to this day I vividly recall his caring manner. It created intense loyalty and admiration. His bedside visit reaffirmed everything he said he would do before the operation.

The last time I purchased a car, the salesperson encouraged me to call him when it would need servicing.

"Just let me know in advance," he told me, "and you can take my car until yours is ready." Sure enough, he did make that car available. He constantly monitored and updated a "profile" of each of his customers. It was his way of ensuring that he was meeting and satisfying my every expectation.

Never miss an opportunity for a *lagniappe*. It's French. It means "*an unexpected extra.*"

Your utilizing one will really separate you from the competition. Send your customers a personal thank-you note for their time. Or a letter of congratulations if you hear of their promotion. Or a small gift.

Lagniappes create a sense of loyalty with your customers and can also provide a strong incentive for more *frequent* purchases.

If these tools are so simple to use, then why don't more people use them--to their advantage? Perhaps they are lazy, or they don't realize it takes extra effort.

Many of us are afraid to contact customers after a sale. Until I trained the sales force of one business, its staff rarely contacted customers even though they knew exactly when their purchase had been delivered.

"If something was wrong," they told me, "we don't have time to get involved." My reply: Make it your business to *want* to call them.

Should you uncover a problem, you will have an opportunity to solve it!

The Washington Direct Selling Education Foundation released a important statistic from the Technical Assistant Research Program. It found that 96 percent of all dissatisfied customers never complain directly to a business.

Instead, they buy elsewhere.

When they do, however, they complain to as many as 10 other people.

If you follow up with your customers, you will be in the minority. But you will be acting professionally. You will be developing relationships that will develop your business.

Pay particular attention to your customers at these crucial times:

1. At the initial sale but before your customer leaves your presence.

2. The first 72 hours after the sale has closed.

3. Continual follow-up throughout the year (once you have asked your customers how often they would like you to hear from you.)

4. At the end of the year, with some form of appreciation on your part, ranging from a gift to a thank-you note.

Now list what you are currently doing at these crucial periods.

Practice Exercise:

The salesperson should begin practicing as if a sale has just been closed. Practice reaffirming to your customer that they made the correct decision in buying your product or service.

Customer Follow-up Worksheet

Date:

Name:

Street Address:

City: State: Zip:

Telephone: Secretary/Receptionist:

• Decision Maker   • Influencer   • Other

• Hot   • Definite immediate interest

               • Intends to act in 3 months or less

               • Wants additional contact

               • Definite future interest

• Warm   • Intends to act in 3 to 6 months

               • Gathering information

               • Definite interest

• Fair   • Intends to act in 12 or more months

               • Keep on prospect list

Date called   Results/Evaluation   Follow-up

Comments/Additional Information

Chapter 11

Tool #9

"Turning Over"

Few people in business realize the value of "turning over"--asking for the assistance of another sales associate who is best suited during a particular moment to bring closure.

Instead, they sell under the notion: "If I can't close this deal, or handle this problem myself, well then no one else around here can either."

How foolish!

This kind of attitude is unnecessary. Most of all, it harms the success and prosperity of an entire organization.

In contrast, wise companies encourage their salespeople to drop this "I-can-do-it-all" attitude. It should be a TEAM effort. Together, everyone achieves more. When they do, their sales will increase. It's simple: They have maximized business from their customers.

The results will go right to their bottom line.

That finding may not have convinced you. Then perhaps your answering this question will:

"What would happen to my company if every day, or if every week, each of my sales personnel made just *one additional sale?*"

Over a full year, one incremental sale each day or each week will benefit companies far more than they could ever imagine!

For this reason, I always focus on consistently unsuccessful sales efforts when I begin to counsel my clients.

First, I review a recent list of prospects one of their salespeople has called upon. Even this review takes some doing. The feeling is that if one salesperson has failed, then no one else in the company should try. This attitude ignores the fact that circumstances for selling may unexpectedly be more favorable during a second attempt.

Then I present the prospect list to another associate within the same company. I ask the person to follow up.

Invariably, after making contact with every prospect on the original list, that new person manages to close at least one sale.

Clients are delighted with the results.

They also discover a flaw in their respective companies.

Most salespeople protect their own turf at the expense of closing more sales. Equally damaging, they don't consider themselves members of a cohesive team.

Surprised?

Haven't I said that it takes 13 times to learn a new communication and at least 113 times to begin to change a behavior?

"If I 'turn over,'" one salesperson tells me, "then somebody else will get the commission, not me." My response is that something is better than nothing! What about a split commission?

A colleague will complain: "This is all about my territory; she's not in my territory, so how can you expect me to ever say to her, 'Hey, help me out!'"

Remember that statistic about dissatisfied customers?

Some 96 percent of all dissatisfied customers *never* complain directly to their salesperson. Instead, they vent their frustration to people who otherwise might have become customers of that same business.

What a double dose of trouble for any company in that situation!

Changing this attitude will require nothing less than the total commitment of the front-office. It will require having the entire organization recognize the importance of learning a new sales approach through proper training and practice. It will require salespeople to operate under a new assumption.

This assumption is that one person can never close every customer every time.

We all know this assumption is true. Yet we refuse to "turn over" customers even though this stubbornness has created, in their minds, a "turn off."

However, this result need not repeat itself.

If salespersons actively follow the steps I have already introduced, the entire organization will benefit. If they practice learning to ask and to listen, they will discover their customers' real needs. When that approach exposes an objection, they will uncover the real reason for customer resistance.

Something else.

When everyone in a company accepts the notion of "turning over," it will give the organization a new perspective on its overall approach to selling.

It may be that the salesperson is uncomfortable with a particular customer. Or it could be that the salesperson doesn't have enough experience or doesn't know enough about a particular product. Or the prospective client may just be having a bad day.

For example, a salesperson may realize she lacks certain qualifications to sell a specific product or service. Or they may sense for some reason that, during a trial close, a prospect becomes uncomfortable with her personality or with her business attire. It could even be something intangible.

At this point, an organization that has learned to think of itself as a unit with diverse levels of skill and talent will gain a competitive edge. What's more, its associates will know precisely when to deploy the person who will be most responsive to a particular customer.

If it is not the first salesperson a customer has encountered from the same company, all the better.

Therefore, a wise associate will decide to turn over. They will give the customer a sincere reason for involving a fellow associate.

At a follow-up meeting they will introduce the associate. In the presence of that individual, they will explain the rationale for the change. It could be the person recently handled a sale with a similar buyer. It may be that the associate's experience, or personality, is a better match.

At that point, as a professional, the first salesperson will leave.

If done properly, everyone will benefit. A company that believes in this practice will have established policies that encourage associates to split commissions. Turning over will foster stronger customer relationships. It will show clients that it cares about them.

A company that "turns over" at the right moment is really *turning on* sales *and* maintaining good rapport. And that's 90% of the battle!

Now, be sure to *practice* these guidelines for turning over:

1. Decide to turn over.

2. Give the customer a sincere reason for involving another sales associate.

3. Identify the appropriate associate who will take over in your place.

4. Introduce the associate to the customer.

5. In front of the customer, explain the details of the situation to the associate. Involve the customer in the interaction.

6. Leave.

Practice Exercise:

Practice turning over as if you are involved in
the three situations I have already cited in this
chapter. Once this turning over has been
accomplished, stop and provide feedback to the
participant.

Chapter 12
Tool #10

Handling Difficult Customers

Research on dissatisfied customers has a bright side.

The same survey conducted by the Technical Assistant Research Program had another surprising finding. Its research revealed that 95 percent of the respondents said they would continue to deal with the company if their complaints were handled to their satisfaction within an acceptable amount of time.

The point is that a complaint provides an opportunity for professional salespersons. Long ago, these professionals learned the value of keeping in regular touch with their customers. They are not afraid to ask their customers about the products or services they have purchased. They want to know if what they have provided has met or exceeded expectations.

If it hasn't, at least they know they still have an opportunity to do something about it.

As you build your base, approach your customers in the same way.

Think of them as members of a "family." Your follow-up will make a difference. It will show your customers you care about them.

This approach will lead to repeat business and referrals.

If you do encounter a difficult customer, always handle their complaint with tact, courtesy and skill. Try not to respond strictly "by the book." In other words, don't be "penny wise but pound foolish" by strictly adhering to company policy.

Be flexible if it means preventing the loss of a customer.

Here are some useful guidelines to follow. I feel the first seven are especially important for everyone within a company or organization, regardless of their area of responsibility.

1. Listen and paraphrase.

2. Apologize.

3. Show empathy.

4. Thank the customer for bringing this complaint to your attention.

5. Reassure the customer that you will do everything possible to resolve their concern.

6. Discuss the situation away from other customers or associates.

7. Get the facts.

8. Solve the problem.

9. Turn over the customer to an associate, if necessary.

10. Most of all, give the customer an unexpected extra to show you appreciate the extra time that he had to devote to this problem.

Stay cool, use a soft tone of voice, and assure your customers you want to solve their problem.

Most of all, don't turn the discussion into an "*I win, you lose*" confrontation. And if you feel you are becoming defensive, it's time to turn over to an associate.

Practice Exercise:

Review current customer-service complaints
and use them as practice scenarios. Also discuss what
your team can do to prevent these situations from
happening again.

Conclusion

This book pulls no surprises.

Nor does it offer any slick tricks.

Instead, the selling tools it introduces represent what I have learned from assisting some of America's most dynamic companies and successful entrepreneurs for a quarter-century.

Others I developed as director of training for J.B. Robinson Jewelers, one of the nation's fastest-growing retailers in the 1970s and 80s.

Each of these 10 professional sales techniques involves practice and preparation. Combined, they will form the foundation of your success in business.

Unlike most of your peers in selling who look for a quick "sales fix," you will be really prepared for your customers.

You will experience increased sales, improved profits, and, most important, professional growth. In fact, I will guarantee it!

Why am I so confident?

That confidence comes from the feedback from clients and participants in my seminars across the country. They tell me that, thanks to their practicing these 10 sales techniques, they experience immediate and sustained improvement in their on-the-job performance. So do others in their companies and organizations.

Now you can apply these techniques yourself. While you still have time.

Need motivation?

How about prospects of flat or slumping sales?

A shrinking market?

Your being expected to suddenly handle a host of new responsibilities that go well beyond your current "job description"?

Rumored consolidation of your company or department?

Heightened job insecurity?

Keener competition from a proliferation of suppliers?

Fewer sales opportunities?

Your customers have less time to hear your presentation?

Or perhaps realizing you must make a "course correction" in your career before it hits dead end?

Selling is not just a job. It's a profession. It is just like teaching, medicine or the law.

When did a caring teacher ever practice on a classroom full of students? Or a doctor on a patient? Or an attorney before a jury and a judge?

How, then, do you begin?

Begin by recognizing that your very livelihood depends on your success in selling. So practicing these 10 successful sales techniques will never be more timely than now.

It will increase your sales. It will improve your productivity.

It will improve the chances of your achieving something the first time.

You will never again have to practice on your customers, especially when you will rarely get a second sales opportunity.

Review Section

Are You Practicing on Your Customers?

Definition of a Professional Sales Person

> Asking, not telling
> Listening, not talking

Seven Qualities that make you a professional

> Active Listening
> Organization
> Persistence
> Confidence
> Enthusiasm
> Sincerity
> Honesty

Ten Practice Topics
(tools of our profession)

1. Working understanding of product & company
2. Greeting customers & establishing rapport
3. Determining need for your products/services
4. Presenting features & benefits of products/services
5. Overcoming objections
6. Closing
7. Introducing "Add-On" opportunities
8. Reaffirming the sale
9. Turning over
10.Handling difficult customers

Topics to Review

1. Ten Benefits of Practice
2. Practice Guidelines
3. Practice Forms
4. Greeting & Rapport Guidelines
5. Steps for Overcoming Objections
6. Steps for Handling Difficult Customers
7. The Twelve Closes

About the Author

Marvin Montgomery is a sales training veteran, with proven success. He has helped turn around hundreds of companies and their sales programs with his sage advice, powerful techniques, and emphasis on practicing before meeting the customer. He is nationally known for his effectiveness.

For over a quarter century, Marvin has taught professional selling techniques to professionals. The list of his students includes thousands of people who have chosen selling as their career, as well as many more who use selling skills as an incidental part of their work.

When he was the director of sales for one of the largest national jewelry chains in the United States, Marvin trained over 1,200 individuals in 95 stores. Other companies benefiting from his work include **Progressive Insurance, Society Bank/Keycorp, TRW, Cleveland Clinic Foundation, E.B. Brown Opticians, Malley's**

Chocolates, law firms, manufacturers, retailers, and service companies.

Marvin consistently earns praise for his unique approaches to sales training. Compliments are commonplace, and highly successful companies attribute their achievement to applying what they learned from this consummate professional.

Marvin Montgomery is a Professional Member of the **National Speakers Association** and presents speeches and seminars for corporations and trade associations throughout the United States and Canada. If you are interested in learning more about his speeches or his two-day interactive workshops you may reach him through his corporate office:

Marvin E. Montgomery & Associates
3718 Concord Drive
Cleveland, Ohio 44122
(216) 591-1930
FAX (216) 464-5556

George A. Becker is president of George A. Becker & Co., a public relations firm based in Cleveland, Ohio.

Ask your local bookseller for any of these Oakhill Press Titles or order direct.
1 (800) 322-6657

Can I Have 5 Minutes of Your Time? ISBN 0-9619590-7-X
Dozens of useful ideas to help you be more effective, increase sales and keep customers. This compact, easy-to-read book by Hal Becker, Xerox Corporation's highest ranked salesperson, combines great ideas with funny and useful anecdotes to entertain *and* boost sales. $12.95 paperback.

Keeping Good People ISBN 0-9619590-9-6
Reducing employee turnover is a serious, bottom line issue. Keep your good employees, and keep them happy and productive with the scores of strategies you'll find in Roger Herman's best-selling book. Featured by *Business Week* and Newbridge Executive Book Clubs. $15.00 paperback.

Overcoming the Overwhelming ISBN 0-9619590-4-5
Providing practical inspiration and hope to those who face adversity, Charles King's book is not another hackneyed look at positive thinking. Anyone facing serious challenges and setbacks will benefit from this book! $9.95 paperback.

The Process of Excelling
This concise, how-to management book is designed to help managers empower their people to "excelling," Roger Herman sets forth the twelve essential elements of successful team leadership. Great ideas for leaders in the 90s.$12.95 paperback

More Oakhill Press Titles to boost your productivity!

Speaking Magic   ISBN 0-9619590-8-8
Easy-to-master, practical exercises. A step-by-step program for becoming a more effective speaker. Perfect for business professionals who must address *any* type of audience, Carolyn Dickson's book provides techniques for improving vocal skills, creating stage presence and developing your own unique, dynamic style. $12.95 paperback.

Turbulence! Challenges and Opportunities in the World of Work   ISBN 1-886939-01-2
Are you prepared for the dramatic changes that are coming in the world of work? That preparation could mean the difference between your future success or failure! Roger Herman's most recent book describes trends in motion right now, the critical factors to watch and what you can expect in the workplace, workforce and workstyles of the next 5-15 years. $22.95 hardcover.

"When it comes to books, Oakhill Press means Business!"